Victorian and Edwardian
ESSEX
from old photographs

1 *(overleaf)*   Boxall's Tea Rooms at Lambourne End near Romford

Victorian and Edwardian

ESSEX

from old photographs

Introduction and commentaries by

STAN JARVIS

B. T. BATSFORD LTD

LONDON

Books by Stan Jarvis: *In Search of Essex* (with Colin Harrison); *Discovering Essex*; *Discovering Christian Names*; *Blake House Farm* and other works of local history.

B. T. Batsford Ltd
4 Fitzhardinge Street, London W1
Printed and bound in Great Britain by
William Clowes & Sons, Limited London, Beccles and Colchester
First published in 1973
ISBN 0 7134 0127 3
Text copyright © Stan Jarvis 1973

CONTENTS

I dedicate this book to my mother
Evelyn A. Jarvis
in appreciation of her loving care
and her heart-warming encouragement

ACKNOWLEDGMENTS

The list which follows shows clearly the extent to which I am indebted to others in the compilation of this book, but there are some people I would like to mention separately as objects of my especial gratitude.

The staff of the Students' Room and the Photographic Department of the Essex Record Office, Miss Jane Dansie, Reference Librarian of Chelmsford Public Library, the staff of the Visual and Aural Aids Service of Essex County Council and the photographers of the Essex Chronicle.

All these kind people helped me far beyond the bounds of their official capacities.

There are those people who responded to my appeals and sent in so many photographs. It would not be possible to mention every sender by name, but I would particularly mention the Misses Norfolk of Elmstead Market for their helpfulness and hospitality.

This list of photographs and their origin is of itself an expression of thanks: nos. 1–6, 11–26, 28–35, 37, 41–42, 47, 50–55, 57–59, 62–72, 74–80, 85, 87–89, 91–92, 94–101, 103, 105–112, 114, 116–120, 122, 129, 131, 133–137, 140–141, 145–150, and 152 from The Essex Record Office; nos. 7–10, 39, 48–49, 60, 90, 94–97, 124–127, 130, 138–139, 142, and 144 from Chelmsford Public Library; nos. 27, 56, and 128 from Sir John Elliot; no. 36 from the late Mrs. K. Boreham; nos. 38, and 43–46 from Mr. Evan Mead; no. 40 from Dr. M. R. Nott; nos. 61, and 121 from Mr. R. W. Smith; nos. 73, 81–82, 84, 86, 104, 113, 132, and 143 from the Misses Norfolk; no. 83 from the Publishers; no. 93 from Mr. Derek C. Marshall; no. 102 from Mr. A. C. Parsonson, J.P.; no. 115 from Mrs. W. G. Wright; no. 123 from Mr. Paul Tritton; no. 151 from the late Mr. Frank Howland.

INTRODUCTION

Who owned the first camera in Essex? What a tremendous stir it must have caused – and all that excitement has gone quite unrecorded. Since the invention, in 1835, of the photographic process as we know it today, millions of photographs have been taken in Essex alone, but it is hard to come by the earlier specimens.

The earliest surviving photographs that could be traced for this work are of the eighteen-sixties. From the 'eighties the trickle becomes a flood and selection becomes the difficulty.

Photography has been made such an easy art today that we forget the time and trouble which had formerly to be taken to get a picture at all. People and objects had to be motionless while the photograph was being taken so that they did not blur the image while the plate slowly developed.

Another kind of development, almost too rapid, is changing the county from an agricultural area to a residential and industrial complex, and making it hard to imagine just what Essex looked like only 70 years ago. In old photographs the original, and much more rural, character of the county is strikingly brought out.

The task of recreation becomes easier if there is a library to hand, replete with records of the period, especially newspapers. The files of the *Essex Chronicle* and the *Essex Weekly News,* preserved on microfilm in the Chelmsford Public Library, are a fascinating key to the thoughts and actions of Essex people over the last 200 years.

The original documents collected together in the Essex Record Office are in the handwriting of the people of the time. They continue through a thousand years up to the date of documents written or signed by some of the very people who appear in these photographs.

There is also a great store of reminiscence. A certain nostalgia often suffuses the picture it provides, a slight blurring of the focus which makes good things better and bad things, well – all for the best in the end. Rider Haggard, however, in his *Rural England,* questioned an Essex farm worker on life in the 'sixties, and made his unbiased report: 'Not far from Blunt's Hall I saw an old labourer named John Lapwood, whose life experience, which I verified by enquiry, is worth preserving. For half a century or more he worked on the Post Hall and Oliver Farms in Witham, and now, by the help of some kind friends, was spending his last days

in a little cottage, where he lived with his wife . . .
He told me that in his young days wages for horsemen
used to be down to 9s. a week, and for daymen to 8s.,
when the weather allowed them to be earned. During
the Crimean War, bread cost him a shilling a loaf, and
other food a proportionate price. He stated that for
months at a time he had existed upon nothing but a
diet of bread and onions, washed down, when he was
lucky, with a little small-beer. These onions he ate
until they took the skin off the roof of his mouth,
blistering it to whiteness, after which he was obliged
to soak them in salt to draw 'the virtue' out of them.
They had no tea, but his wife imitated the appearance
of that beverage by soaking a burnt crust of bread in
boiling water . . .'

It is not surprising that the searching poverty of
such times was not reflected in contemporary photographs; though the romantic character of the 'old
farm labourer' became popular at the end of the
century. John Lapwood's life contrasted with that
of the village doctor of Tolleshunt D'Arcy, the
celebrated Dr Salter who recorded in his diary in
1873: 'Nov 6. At Rainham coursing meeting my blood
carried off everything. I had a spill from a horse and
got rather bruised – he fell into a blind ditch on top of

me and then trod on my head . . . Nov 18. A heavy day's work. In the evening I went in to Chelmsford to see 'A living skeleton', who was being exhibited at a twopenny show. I was much interested, and requested to have a private interview with him in the morning, which request was readily granted by the showman . . . Nov 19. Up early and had a most interesting interview with the skeleton, who had a huge breakfast and seemed to enjoy it . . . It was such an extraordinary case that I sent him to the College of Surgeons and other scientific places in London, and he got a considerable income by going to various societies and being examined in various ways. Dec 19. A Trades Union agitator addressed the labourers of the village, and met with some warm opposition. He and I had an altercation in which he came off second best.'

The doctor and his animals were much photographed, for he could afford the services of a commercial photographer. The collections in the Essex repositories, and in private hands, reflect this commercial attitude to photography. Scenes of the hunt, big house family groups, posed portraits – all are available in embarrassing quantity. The work of the more purely artistic photographer has seldom been preserved.

There are many events which should, one would have thought, have been photographed as matters of mere record, yet no photographs exist. Take a classic example. Epping Forest might have been chopped down and developed as a London suburb had it not been for strong local opposition. Its preservation was ensured and it was formally declared open to the public by Queen Victoria on 6th May 1882. Yet not a single photograph of that occasion appears to exist in Essex. One possible reason for this and other omissions is that until the invention of the half-tone process for the printing of photographs in newspapers, an artist was retained to draw a sketch from the photograph so that a suitable engraving could be made for the press. The photograph then would be cast aside, its intermediary function fulfilled.

The coming of the railway in the 'thirties and 'forties of the last century was the greatest single factor in the urbanisation of Essex. The very early photographer in Kelvedon was able to show the amazing emptiness of the roads (Plate 30) where weeds were beginning to grow. The endless expansion of London had its effect on the south west of the county. Yet hay carts could still be seen in Stratford Broadway at the end of the century, taking food for cows still kept in yards and outhouses to keep up London's milk supply.

Large estates were still to be found further north where, from the eighties on the landed gentry posed, and had their staff pose for the camera. The occasion came to be something of a status symbol. The photograph, and the impedimenta and ritual involved in its production still proved a novelty sufficient to draw people into self-conscious posturing for the pleasure of perpetuating their image.

In Essex a great many such photographs had to be sifted before the glitter of that golden find, an unsophisticated snapshot gave encouragement to this compiler. Through the mass of photographs, stiffly posed or casually caught, the name of Spalding is constantly repeated. Without Frederick Spalding's contribution a book like this could hardly be completed. He was born in 1858 and died in 1947. In the interval after his death and the sale of the premises thousands of glass negatives lay in his shop in Chelmsford High Street, to be swept away unceremoniously by 'developers'.

But some negatives were saved, and from all over the county photographs by the ubiquitous Spalding have, over the years, flowed back to the library and record office in the county town. From his shop

Frederick Spalding travelled about indefatigably. He built up an enormous collection of views to be reproduced as postcards for sale in his gift shop. In the production of these photographs Spalding added his individual, rather endearing touches. Where he felt the sky was all too intrusive over a broad view of Essex marshland he would add a few birds in flight – or many, according to his whim, all carefully drawn in on the negative. Later he even drew in an aeroplane to add interest to a wedding group.

Village streets in the days before the motor car looked wide and empty, especially as foregrounds to popular postcards. Spalding solved the problem by positioning willing village lads all down the street, and photographing them in an eternal game of leap-frog! This ploy is almost Spalding's trade mark in numerous Essex village scenes (Plate 21).

But this was a harmless enough practice and Spalding made a wonderful job of the finished photograph. He could command a pose from the Prince of Wales in distinguished company at the Earl of Warwick's place at Great Easton (Plate 54) seemingly as easily as getting a gaggle of girls and boys to do a dance in front of the school at Woodham Mortimer (Plate 134).

There are anonymous masterpieces to be found, even reproduced as postcards, which prove the claim of photography to rank high in the art of portraiture. Spalding's wonderful portrait of Charlie Sweeting (Plate 39) is matched by C. S. Tyler's picture of the blacksmith at Earls Colne (Plate 111).

Some photographs are valuable as 'firsts', whatever their composition or physical shape. One such is the game of tennis (Plate 148), photographer unknown, date a matter of conjecture, but it is the first photograph of tennis in Essex so far discovered. If on the other hand the temptation to include many early photographs of football teams had to be resisted, not a single early action photograph of football was found. The difficulty of recording a moving object had not then been solved successfully, but the solution was just around the corner.

THE TOWN

2 Wood Street, Walthamstow, about 1902. The stables near Clock House in this street, owned at the time by Mr Vince, were in use up to 1940

3   Walthamstow *c.* 1907. Looking towards St James Street Station railway bridge. Trams were introduced on 3rd June 1905 and the lines were finally removed in 1939

4 Romford High Street *c.* 1905. On the left the chemist 'by appointment to the Household of H.R.H. Princess Eulalia' gave the local rendezvous 'Lasham's corner'. Next to it is the London and County Bank and then the White Hart. On the other side of the road the old Corn Exchange is now Woolworth's

5 North Street, Romford *c.* 1910. Every building in this photograph has been demolished. The old Congregational church had already become the offices of the *Romford Recorder*. The trees in the background stood in Marshall's Park, a private estate now entirely developed

6   Moulsham Street, Chelmsford, just after 1902, when the Co-operative stores on the left were opened by the Countess of Warwick. The Methodist church across the old Stone Bridge replaced the famous Cock Inn in 1898, and has in turn been replaced by Cater's super-market

7   Shire Hall, Chelmsford at the turn of the century. The gun, a trophy of the Crimean War, now stands in Oaklands Park. On the right hand side, Fred Spalding's photography business carried on until about 1958. This is one of the hundreds of photographs he took all round the county

8   Tindal Square, Chelmsford, 1880. Nicholas Conyngham Tindal was born in Chelmsford and in 1776 became Chief Justice of the Court of Common Pleas. In 1857 this, the only statue in the county town, was erected to his memory

9 Tindal Square, Chelmsford, 1874. Wagons brought in from the country to take back beer and provisions for 'Harvest Home' are being guarded by farm labourers, while their fellow-workers tour the town on horseback collecting 'largesse' or tips from traders who dealt with their employers

10 *(overleaf)*   The old conduit head in Chelmsford High Street about 1890. It stood originally where the Tindal statue now stands outside the Shire Hall and marked the outflowing of the stream piped across the fields from the Burgess well which was the town's first water supply. By 1940 it had become such an obstruction to traffic that it was removed to Tower Gardens

11 Looking up Colchester's High Street to the Town Hall just after its opening on 15th May 1902 by the Earl of Rosebery. The unusual tower behind the Union Jack is a water tower built in 1882 and known from that year as 'Jumbo' after the popular elephant sold to Barnum and Bailey's circus. The George on the right is a coaching inn which still retains its eighteenth-century façade

12 Maldon High Street c. 1909. The clock marks the fifteenth-century Moot Hall with its portico of 1830. The clock itself was presented to the town by George Courtauld, of the great weaving family, in 1881

13 Halstead around 1905

14 Southend-on-Sea: hardware in 1910. Frederick Elkins, oil and colour man, had his name boldly painted in when he took over this hardware business at 56, Rectory Grove. By 1937 the trade of 'Italian warehouseman' had disappeared entirely from the county directory

15 Epping on market day some time before 1906, when, Kelly's Directory says, 'Epping has a weekly market on Friday, which is well attended and 13th and 14th November (Holland Fair), also for cattle and horses.'

16 Thaxted High Street from Mill End, 1900. The parish church is one of the finest in Essex, benefiting from the prosperous wool and cutlery trade in the locality. The guildhall below it, facing down the street, is 500 years old. The street is in almost every respect of the same appearance today

17   Saffron Walden High Street about 1908. The Abbey Hotel was still running as a commercial hotel up to the last war. On the right the sign of the Cross Keys is partly visible. Since this photograph the plaster exterior has been removed to expose the timber-work

18   Braintree High Street in 1910. The Horn Hotel continues with little external alteration. The imposing pillared building supporting the clock is the Corn Exchange built in 1839 and enlarged in 1877

19 Chipping Hill, Witham, in 1900. The cart awaits the horse that has been taken into the forge for shoeing. There is a blacksmith still in business in these premises which, like the cottages on the green behind, remain substantially unaltered. The tool leaning against the wall is a cart-jack for removing wheels

DOWN THE ROAD

20 The White Horse, Widford, 1887: a good deal altered but still on the same site today. The man standing by the window is holding an auger for making holes for fence posts

21 Writtle, 1890. Looking from the Cock and Bell across St John's Green. The Victorian jubilee lamp standard on the granite pedestal has been removed. Behind the far right-hand corner of the green Marconi sited his research establishment from which the first radio broadcasts in this country emanated

22 Chigwell. The King's Head, a Dickensian inn. 'The old King's Head looks as inviting as the day Dickens selected it as the Maypole in ''Barnaby Rudge''' (published in 1841). The stucco has been removed following the modern fashion of exposing the timbers

23   Danbury, 1890. One of the highest points in the county. The Griffin flourishes yet and the post office continues in the cottage with the telegraph office sign

24 Audley End village about 1900. Though eclipsed by the great house named after it the village offers in this street the sight of a sixteenth-century row of almshouses which, after the last war, were saved from demolition by being converted into a home for retired clergy of the Church of England

25 Woodham Walter: the Bell Inn, 1890. A typical Essex village pub in what was then an isolated community

26 *(overleaf)* Writtle village pond, 1905

27 Estelle and Josephine, daughters of R. D. Blumenfeld, some-time editor of the *Daily Express*, are in the trap. Their nanny, Lizzie Drain of Thaxted, leads the donkey on the main Dunmow–Saffron Waldon road in 1905

28 Chipping Ongar's main street about 1902. The gabled clock-tower of the Budworth Hall was added to celebrate the Jubilee of Queen Victoria. All the buildings on the left remain essentially the same as far as the eye can see. Barclays Bank has replaced the shop on the right and the trees in the road have gone

29   Stratford Broadway in the early morning around 1900 when hay carts were still an essential feature of traffic into central London. The granite obelisk in the foreground was designed by J. Bell to commemmorate Samuel Gurney (1786–1856), nineteenth-century Quaker banker and philanthropist

30 Kelvedon High Street, 1870. The railway had taken traffic from the roads on which it was then reported that grass was growing

DOWN THE RIVER

31 Canvey Island, looking towards South Benfleet, 1905. At low tide these stepping stones replace the ferry. A concrete road now crosses the creek on the same line, turning left along the bank where the child is standing on the stile

32 *(overleaf)* Hythe Quay, Colchester, 1900. The port of Colchester from Roman times still had a great deal of coastal barge traffic despite the increasing challenge of the railway

33 Canvey Island. The same creek at high tide, 1905. The bridge which replaced this ferry boat was opened in 1931

34 Benfleet Ferry, looking across to Canvey Island from South Benfleet. The necessarily high sea walls prevent a view of the island. The hay barge and the cattle indicate the 'very rich grazing and some arable land' attributed to the island in the contemporary county guide.

DOWN ON THE FARM

35 Rochford *c.* 1900. The ploughman and his team make an early start

36 Stapleford Abbots. A postcard sent by the young lady on the horse rake to show how she helped with the hay-making while on holiday in 1910

37 A postcard sent from Harlow in 1907. 'This is our M.P. (Lt Col Rt Hon. A. R. M. Lockwood, CVO) speaking after the ploughing match'

38 Isaac Mead, born the son of a farm labourer in 1859, conquered all kinds of adversity to rent his own farm in 1882. This scene of dinner in the harvest field at Waples Mill Farm is a moment of relaxation in months of grinding labour. This and other photographs of the family come through the courtesy of his son Evan Mead

39 Charles Sweeting, born in 1826 near the Pig and Whistle at Chignall St James, spent the whole of his working life as a farm labourer to the Christy's. This photograph taken about 1890 shows him about to enjoy his 'beever' – the Essex farm-hands' 'elevenses'

40 *(overleaf)* Cutting barley in Miltons Field at Great Lodge Farm, Great Bardfield, in 1904. In 1903 the weather was so wet that wheat could not be drilled. The harvesters, from left to right, are: Fred Saines, Arthur Carter, Silas Ruffle, Herbert Allen, Wm. Perkiss, Walter Carter, Jim Carter, Geo. Springett, Chas. Heard, John Broyd, Harry Green

41   A totally male society. Colchester cattle market in 1909, facing the old cottages which lined Sheepen Road, now a car park

42   Another view of the market taken at the same time, looking towards the Balkerne Hill – North Hill junction. The further block of terraced houses has been demolished

43 *(opposite)*   The gaffer, Isaac Mead, appraises the daily egg collection on Waples Mill Farm, Beauchamp Roding in 1909

44 Two more Waples Mill Farm turkeys for Leadenhall Market (. . . a gentleman I know from North Weald asked me how the turkey trade was. I told him, 'Rotten'. He says, 'Do you go into Leadenhall Market, and you will have no difficulty in selling them there:') (Isaac Mead, *Life Story of an Essex Lad*, 1923)

45 Boxing turkeys for the London market at Waples Mill Farm in 1909. 'As my lads grew up and I kept taking more land, there was no one to protect the poultry from foxes, and I was unable to continue.' (Isaac Mead)

46 Isaac Mead was a God-fearing Non-Conformist. By industry and against all kinds of obstacles he obtained his own farm. Such was his love for the place that he had a piece of one of the fields consecrated, that he and his family might rest in peace in the very land which had succoured them in life. Here his two sons are plucking two of the many turkeys he sold on contract to the breweries which distributed them to landlords as Christmas presents

47 The kitchen, Rochford Hall, 1900. From being the sixteenth-century home of Sir Thomas Boleyn and his famous daughter Anne the Hall suffered neglect and partial demolition, until, at this time, it was inhabited by the farm bailiff to the Lord of the Manor. Today it is the local golf clubhouse

THE BIG HOUSE

48 'GRAHAME WHITE'S WEDDING. GUESTS BY AEROPLANE. BRILLIANT
SCENES AT WIDFORD YESTERDAY. . . . the bells in the tower were joyously
pealed. Simultaneously the throb of a powerful engine was heard, and Mr.
Hucks was seen soaring above the church at a tremendous speed. He circled
the Church several times, and then took a wider sweep . . . and eventually came
down (at Hylands) in a beautiful volplane.' (*Essex County Chronicle*, 28 June
1912.) Claude Grahame-White (1879–1959) married Dorothy Taylor of New
York. He was the first Englishman to be granted a certificate of proficiency as an
aviator

49 Sir Daniel Fulthorpe Gooch and his family at Hylands, 1908. The fifty-year-old owner of this, the 'big house' of Widford, has his three-year-old son Robert Douglas on his lap. His wife and their daughter Phyllis Evelyn and son and heir Lancelot Daniel also appear. Hylands was first built about 1728 for Sir John Comyns, passing down the years to the Hanbury family, in whose occupation it was seriously damaged by fire. The house and 433 acres of its parkland have been purchased recently by the town of Chelmsford as a permanent natural open space for its citizens. The future of the house hangs in the balance

50   Interior of Easton Lodge, home of the Earl of Warwick, in the Nineties. Here at Little Easton, an unsophisticated village, Lady Frances Warwick entertained on a scale so grand that one debt of £64,000 was never repaid.

51   The staff at Easton Lodge were devoted to Frances, Countess of Warwick, who in later life was a staunch supporter of the socialist cause and left the mansion to the labour party

52 Easton Lodge. The Prince of Wales and local gentry, guests of the Earl of Warwick. The house has been demolished but the stable block has been converted into houses

53 Easton Lodge. Lady Frances Warwick, a skilful horsewoman, takes the reins. The Prince of Wales sits next to her. She became his 'Darling Daisy' and one of the reasons for an ever-increasing expenditure on lavish entertaining

54 Easton Lodge. The Prince of Wales being entertained by the Earl and Countess of Warwick about 1890. Standing, left to right: Lord Gordon Lennox, Count Menedorff, Lady Eva Greville, HRH The Prince of Wales, Frances, Countess of Warwick, HRH The Duchess of York, HSH the Duchess of Teck. Sitting left to right: HSH Prince Francis of Teck, Lady Lister Kaye, the Earl of Warwick, Lady Lillian Wemyss and Count Soveral

55 17 October 1892. The Prince of Wales at the Blythwood Dairy, Stansted Mountfitchet, the most modern of its kind, opened on this occasion with a golden key. Sir James Blyth (1st Baron Blyth of Stansted Mountfitchet) is leaning over the balcony wearing a hat. His uncle, Sir Charles Gold stands beside him. Another uncle, Sir Walter Gilbey stands beside the Prince with hat in hand. Beside him stands Lady Brooke (Countess of Warwick). Lord Brooke and Lady Blyth stand bottom left and right

TRANSPORT

56 R. D. Blumenfeld, editor of the *Daily Express*, on the main road outside his home, Hill Farm, Great Easton, in about 1905, with his two daughters Estelle and Josephine. The car is an MMC (Motor Manufacturing Company) of which only about 40 were made

57 Colchester. View from the High Street, looking down North Hill in 1905. On the left the Waggon and Horses has become Simkin's, although its façade still declares its ancestry. It is now Adrian's estate agency. The building on the right survives, without its canopy, as the Planet Building Society

58 Coggeshall, meeting place of two bus routes before the First World War. The National Steam Car Company was registered in 1909 to operate the steam buses built for it by the Clarkson-Capel syndicate in Chelmsford. Using the same model, Moore Brothers of Kelvedon operated to Colchester via Coggeshall and were not absorbed by the larger company, now called Eastern National Omnibus Company, until 2 February 1963

59 High Easter 1910. The doctor's car stands in front of his house. It was the village surgery up to a couple of years ago, now it is a private house. After it comes Chapel House and the congregational Chapel with the tower of St Mary's in the distance

60 Chelmsford Railway Station. 1908. This, the second station built since the coming of the railway in 1843, was completed in 1856

61 A traction engine accident in 1908, along the Ongar Road. James and George Matthews had a fleet of such engines to cover the county. Their business continues today

62 A new boiler for Courtauld's silk factory almost at its destination in Halstead as it is drawn up the High Street. Nathan William Pendle's furniture business continued at least up to the last war

63   Billericay High Street in 1900. The White Hart, an eighteenth-century inn, was presided over at this time by the 'tall and stately Bill Punt' in whose family the licence continued over 50 years

AT THE SEASIDE

64 Walton-on-the-Naze in 1895. The contemporary guide-book talks of 'a fashionable healthy and rapidly-rising watering-place', and the hotels can be seen gathering along the top of the cliff. The photograph, taken from the pier, shows the boatmen plying for hire

65 Pierrots at Clacton in 1908. Popplewell and Pullan's Yorkshire Pierrots were a popular summer entertainment on the West Beach. The pier, built in 1871, extends 1,280 feet out to sea

66 Listening to the band at Clacton in 1902. 'In 1899 the Council erected a bandstand on the greensward opposite Colne Road and there military bands . . . played throughout the summer season.' The tree's shape indicates the direction of the prevailing wind

67 Southend in 1900. The scenic railway rising above the trees forms part of the Kursaal erected in 1902

68 Southend in 1898. The mile-and-a-third long pier is claimed to be the longest in the world. From it was taken this view of pleasure boats collecting trippers for a sail down the estuary

69 *(opposite)*   Southend in 1891.

. . . And when (dispos'd for air and prospect fine)
To tread the lofty terrace you incline,
If bright the weather, and the sky serene,
Scarce will you find so beautiful a scene.
The Prince of Rivers with collected force,
In broader channel guides his placid course.
On his proud bosom Commerce swells the sail,
And wafts a various freight with ev'ry gale.
– 'New South-end', by Thomas Archer, 1794

70   Walton-on-the-Naze, 1909: specially developed as a sea-bathing resort in the 1830's after almost total erosion of the earlier village in the eighteenth century. Even the church of All Saints, in the background, is less than a hundred years old

71   Walton-on-the-Naze, 1909. The popularity of the place at this time may be judged by the entry in the 1887 guide: 'A Pier, 800 ft long, extends into the sea. Walton is much frequented in the summer by yachts, and an annual regatta is held in August. During the season, which lasts from June to October, steamers run to and from London, Clacton-on-the-Sea and Harwich.'

72 Wivenhoe at the beginning of the century. In 1884 most of the buildings in the picture were wrecked in the great Essex earthquake. Quay Cottage was rebuilt with the date incorporated as a reminder

EVENTS

73 Elmstead Market. Beating the bounds in 1910: consulting the parish map.
The man with the stick is Mr Martin Whiting. A contemporary account notes
the 'old custom . . . of going round the parish boundaries on Holy Thursday, or
Ascension Day. The school-children, accompanied by the clergymen and parish
officers, walked through their parish from end to end; the boys were switched
with willow wands all along the lines of boundary, the idea being to teach them
to know the bounds of their parish.'

74 Dougal, the notorious 'Moat Farm' murderer, in custody at Saffron Walden railway station in 1903. In 1898 he met Miss Camille Holland, a middle-aged spinster, whom he eventually murdered for her money, burying the body on the farm at Clavering which he had persuaded her to buy. He was hanged at Chelmsford on 14 July 1903

75 Sightseers at the Moat Farm, Clavering where the victim's body was found. It was only after an exhaustive search, including the draining of the moat, that a farm worker happened to mention that Dougal had employed him in filling in a ditch which ran through the farm yard. This was the clue that solved the crime

76 Soldiers relaxing outside the stores at Warley barracks, near Brentwood. All the barracks have now been demolished and a new headquarters for the Ford Motor Company occupies the site

77 Crowds gather to hear George V proclaimed King by the High Sheriff of Essex at Chelmsford on 9 May 1910

78 *(opposite)* Waiting to see the procession of the Dunmow Flitch ceremony in Great Dunmow, 1890. It was a revival of the ancient custom, 'so long connected with Dunmow, of presenting a *Flitch of Bacon* to any couple who, sleeping or waking, had not repented of their marriage for a year and a day. The applicants were required to swear a poetical oath, kneeling on some sharp stones at the church door . . .'

79 Chairing the winners of the Dunmow Flitch – champions of conjugal felicity – about 1900. One of the chairs used can still be seen in Little Dunmow church. The smocks worn by the bearers were the common attire of the previous generation

80 High Easter, 1900. Workmen installing a new water pump on the site of the old village lock-up on the verge of the village street. It stood until recently outside the row of cottages, now one house, called 'Randalls'. Mr Tom Goody from Dunmow, builder, has his hand on the pump

81 Church Parade of the Ancient Order of Foresters Friendly Society at Elmstead Market in 1910. The King's Arms faces across the village green

82 Elmstead Market. Friendly Societies Parade in 1910. Organised by the village baker, Ernest Norfolk. He was a strong supporter of the Ancient Order of Foresters whose members have been accompanied on this church parade by a contingent of the Royal Antediluvian Order of Buffaloes from Colchester. These Friendly Societies, with their schemes of payment for sickness, injury and unemployment were an important part of village life

83 Tea for the old folk at New Hall, Ardleigh in 1912

84 Following the procession after the Church Parade of the Friendly Societies at Elmstead Market in 1910

85 'A ceremonial parade in honour of the King's Birthday by the 3rd Essex (Militia) took place at Chelmsford on Friday. . . . The scene on the parade ground was very picturesque, no prettier setting for the picture being possible than the fine, well-kept (cricket) field, bordered by stately trees. . . . At noon a 'feu de joie' was fired and three hearty cheers were given for the King; while the band played the National Anthem . . .' *(Essex Weekly News.)* The date was 26 June 1908

86 *(opposite)* Elmstead Market. The Royal Antediluvian Order of Buffaloes from Colchester carry their banner in the church parade of 1910

87 Barking Fire Brigade rushing to a fire in 1895. At this time the station was part of the newly-erected Town Hall

88 'The biggest fire which has taken place in Brentwood for a quarter of a century broke out at an early hour on Saturday morning on the premises of Messrs. W. A. Wilson and Company, Great Eastern Stores, High Street; and as a result the whole block of buildings, together with Devonshire House and Roden House, two private houses adjoining, was totally destroyed, the damage being roughly estimated at £20,000.' (*Essex Weekly News,* 10 September 1909.) The granite obelisk of the William Hunter memorial was cracked by the intense heat

89 The Wilson Company fire at Brentwood in 1909. Though the fire was first noticed at about 6 a.m. the clock kept working until a few minutes before the collapse of the tower

90 *(overleaf)* The great flood at Chelmsford on 2 August 1888 when the rivers Chelmer and Can overflowed and inundated the town centre. This scene in the Friars was re-enacted in 1958, since when a flood relief scheme has ended such tragedies. Every building in this picture has been demolished, including the British National Schools on the left and the fourteenth-century cottages at the end of the street marking the entrance to the old friary. The road itself has been renamed as it has been developed to form a dual carriageway ring road

91 'TERRIBLE RAILWAY DISASTER AT WITHAM STATION. ELEVEN PERSONS KILLED AND OVER FORTY INJURED. An accident of appalling character occurred to the Cromer Express at Witham on Friday morning . . . as it passed under the road bridge on the Chelmsford side of the station something went wrong, and in less than a minute the express was hopelessly wrecked and the usually quiet junction was the scene of the most awful confusion and disaster.' (*Essex Weekly News,* 8 September 1905)

OFFICIAL APPEARANCES

92 The 'Ariel' bicycle is known to have been in use by members of the 'Amateur Bicycle Club' in 1870. The rider is probably an employee of one of the express delivery companies flourishing at that time. Posed in Frederick Spalding's studio at Chelmsford

93 *(opposite)* The old 2nd Battalion Volunteers, Essex Regiment. Lewis William Pettitt, 2nd from left at the back, served from 1894–1908

94 The Judge's carriage before a car was introduced in 1906. With two more horses it would be identical with a print of 1762 showing the Judge proceeding up Chelmsford High Street to open the Assize

95 Coachmen and trumpeters who manned the Judge's carriage when he attended the Assize in 1906

96 Turn out of the fire engine at Chelmsford to honour the Mayor on the day in September 1888 that the county town at last obtained its charter of incorporation as a borough. Leading is Percy Butler, whose father, standing by the engine, was the 'resident secretary'

97 The entire Essex County police force at their headquarters in Chelmsford. Seated in the middle of the front row is Capt J. B. B. McHardy, RN, appointed first Chief Constable of the county in 1839. He held the office for more than 40 years

WORK

98   The coalman stops in St Mary's Lane, Upminster about 1900. The place is known as Bell's Corner today from the name of the hotel

99 Taken before 1870 in Kelvedon, the picture shows a shop premises being converted. The number of men employed on such a job surprises us today. This is one of many photographs taken by Sir Thomas Burch Western's bailiff with a very early camera

100 Writtle Brewery in 1900. All evidence of it has disappeared and the site is now occupied by Writtle Garage

101 Kelvedon High Street, 1906. Labourers trenching for drainage or water supply

102 Stephen Arthur Parsonson (second from right) with his son Arthur, was the last of the Colchester basket makers (at 21, North Hill) in 1908. He specialised in oyster skeps for the Colchester oyster fishery and bottle covers for the stone jars used by local breweries

103 Postcard superscribed, 'Harold Wood 9.40, 1/7/10. This view was taken on Sunday. Notice the Superintendent on platform.' Being on the main London–Colchester line maintenance was of the utmost importance

104 Elmstead Market Post Office. Morning delivery, 7 a.m., 1909. Postmaster Mr T. W. Brown. His son Will Brown is on the far right. The 'S' on the chimney is a reminder of the great earthquake in 1884

105 Thaxted Post Office, Town Street, about 1900, under the sub-postmastership of G. Colquhoun Johnston. Deliveries were at 7.30 a.m., 9.0 a.m. and 1.35 p.m.

106 *(previous page)* The quay at Bradwell Riverside in 1910. Loading a cargo of grain or seed on the barge *Mayflower* for a trip round the coast to London

107 The brickfield at Hogg Lane, Grays Thurrock in 1910

VILLAGE CRAFTS

108   The village smithy at Hockley in 1900.

109 Arthur Cottee, the corn dealer and village baker at Stock, in 1880. The 1937 county directory still shows an Arthur Cottee as baker and parish clerk

111 *(opposite)* The village smithy, Earls Colne. The hand holding the bolt, suspended in the window, is probably a trade sign inherited from his predecessors. The picture was produced as a postcard in about 1902 by C. S. Tyler, who was the village chemist and photographer until the First World War

110 The cycle shop in Coggeshall about 1908. Changing fashions are shown in the shape of the handlebars of the young man's bicycle and those of the two new machines offered for sale

112   The wheelwright at Great Bentley, where the village green, the largest in the country, covers 42 acres

113   Wheelwright's shop and yard in the 'eighties at Elmstead Market

114 Charles Partridge, baker's roundsman for H. Carter and Sons of Great Baddow, who, in that small village also carried on the businesses of corn merchants, dairymen, provision merchants and confectioners (1909)

115   Mrs Hannah Wright of Maldon, born in 1845, seen in about 1905 making fishing nets by hand

THE MILLER

116 Stambridge Mill *c*. 1905. Originally a water mill on the Broomhill or Roche river, it was converted to steam and then to electricity by Rankin's, well-known Essex millers. It was burnt down on Sunday, 25 April 1965

117 Heybridge Mill in 1910. As Pevsner said in 1965, it forms 'a pretty picture of small Georgian red brick miller's house and weatherboarded mill-house.'

118 St Osyth. A rare tidal mill seen in 1900. Built in 1718 on the foundations of an earlier building, it was working up until 1930

119 Collecting flour from Bulford Mill, Cressing, about 1900. The mill stands out into the lane from Black Notley to Cressing Station, making it one of the most dangerous bends in the county

120 *(overleaf)* Hornchurch Mill in 1910, when it was run by William Henry Beard, who was also the local baker. One of his carts is seen in the picture

121 *(opposite)*   James and George Matthews' Harold Wood Mills, *c.* 1908. The building was put up in 1905 to house the very latest in steam-driven mills

122   Bringing flour up from Littlebury water mill on the river Cam, or Granta, in 1906

123   The miller, James Martin, parades his family at Howe Street water mill, Great Waltham, at the turn of the century

CHARACTERS

124   This waggoner from Rettendon has now disappeared from memory completely. Only his photograph (taken just before 1910) survives, and his constantly repeated remark – recorded in Spalding's memoirs – 'Gimme 'osses, say I, and 'ang they motorcars!'

125 Labourers in Wells and Perry's brewery at Chelmsford, 1864. S. Hills in the short smock, T. Shonk in the long smock, Jos. Isabel in the fustian jacket

126 *Fine hot pies*
     All rich and ready
     One for a penny!
     Fine hot pies

So cried Richard Hasler on market days in Chelmsford. He was familiarly known as Dick the Pieman, and so well liked that his friends got together to buy him a new 'can' in which the pies were kept warm. Dick was born in 1816 and died in 1876. His father fought at Waterloo

127 Corporal Thomas Bausor of the 4th Essex Chelmsford Volunteers. He was probably the same man who kept the Red Cow Temperance Hotel (now Barclays bank), Broomfield Road, Chelmsford, in the last years of the nineteenth century.

128 H. G. Wells with his wife Jane and on the left Mrs Blumenfeld, wife of the one-time editor of the *Daily Express* (pointing) with a friend – all acting in a charade at Hill Farm, Great Easton, 1910–1911

SCHOOL DAYS

129 King Edward VI School, Chelmsford in 1907. The grammar school moved from its old site in the town to the new building in Broomfield Road in 1890

130 Great Leighs village school in 1908. George With, on the left, was master at this time. His wife and son are on the right

131 Brentwood School, *c.* 1909. At this time there were just 118 boys under the headmastership of the Reverend Edwin Bean, MA

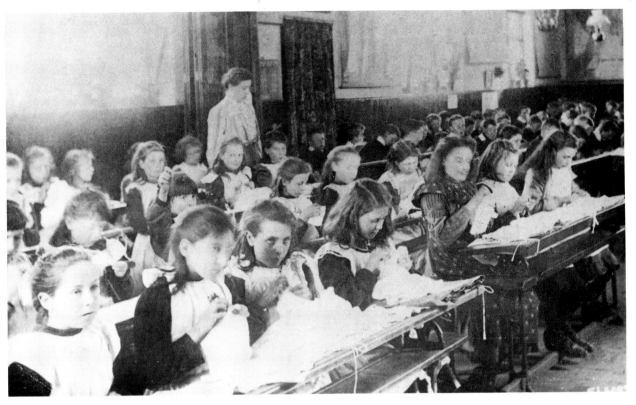

132 More than 100 children in the one-room school at Elmstead Market in 1910

133 The class in shoe repairing at the Essex Industrial School and Home for Destitute Boys, Chelmsford in 1900. The Home was established in 1872. 'The cases admitted are those of a voluntary character and of boys unconvicted of crime sent under a magistrate's order. . . . the boys' time is divided between instruction in school and industrial labour, such as house and garden work, shoemaking, tailoring, laundry and carpentering.'

134 Woodham Walter village school in 1890. The posed game of leap frog is characteristic of Fred Spalding's pictures of village children

135 Cricket at Felsted School in 1910

136   The Chemical Laboratory in King Edward VI School at Chelmsford in 1906

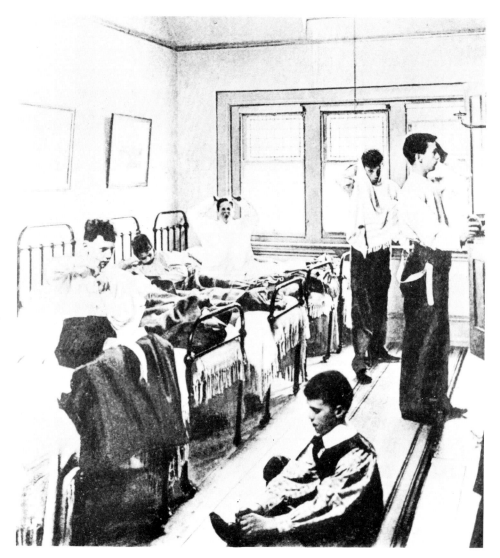

137 King Edward VI School, Chelmsford, from a postcard dated 1907. 'The School has a yearly income of about £300 and under the scheme of the Endowed School Commissioners, 1873, was constituted a second grade school for the education of boys up to the age of 19, and there are now 150, the school being full and 3 new class rooms are in course of erection.' – (*Kelly's Directory*, 1906)

PLAY

138   A fête at Chelmsford in aid of, and in the grounds of the Industrial School
and Home for Destitute Boys in June 1904

139 Chelmsford Cycling Club outside the Saracen's Head, High Street, in the Nineties

140 Essex cyclists meet at Woodford on 22 June 1907 to take part in a competition for fancy dress and decorated bicycles

141 The Chelmsford Ladies Cycling Club in 1890

142 County Meet of Essex cyclists at Chelmsford on 6 June 1883. The member of Parliament, James Round, stands between the second and third posts from the left

143 Bill Taylor (*centre*) and the Reverend Leonard Fenn are there to see fair play at the Elmstead & Great Bromley Horticultural Show cycle race in 1910

144   County Athletic Meeting at Chelmsford on 20 July 1901

145   Bures Hamlet in 1908: the hunt followers outside the Eight Bells

146 Writtle Brewery Football Club, 1880

147 A postcard, sent as a birthday greeting in 1908, shows the Rectory Rangers quoits club of Beaumont

148 Tennis in the early 1900's

149 *(overleaf)* Miss Belle White, Olympic diving champion in 1912, at Braintree Baths when they were opened at Rosehill in 1914

150 A pair-in-hand about to set off from the Cock, Epping in 1908. The Old Thatched House inn just down the road still stands, though both hostelries have been much altered and buildings have sprouted between them

151 Local lads outside the Red Lion, Stebbing, on Bonfire Night in 1888. They so disliked the local policeman, PC Rover, that they burnt his effigy. He was removed that day and a new constable appointed, according to local legend

152 Boxall's Tea Rooms at Lambourne End near Romford. Mrs Ellen Boxall kept generations of London trippers refreshed in their wanderings around the 314 acre woodland – remnant of the great forest of Hainault